AF575421

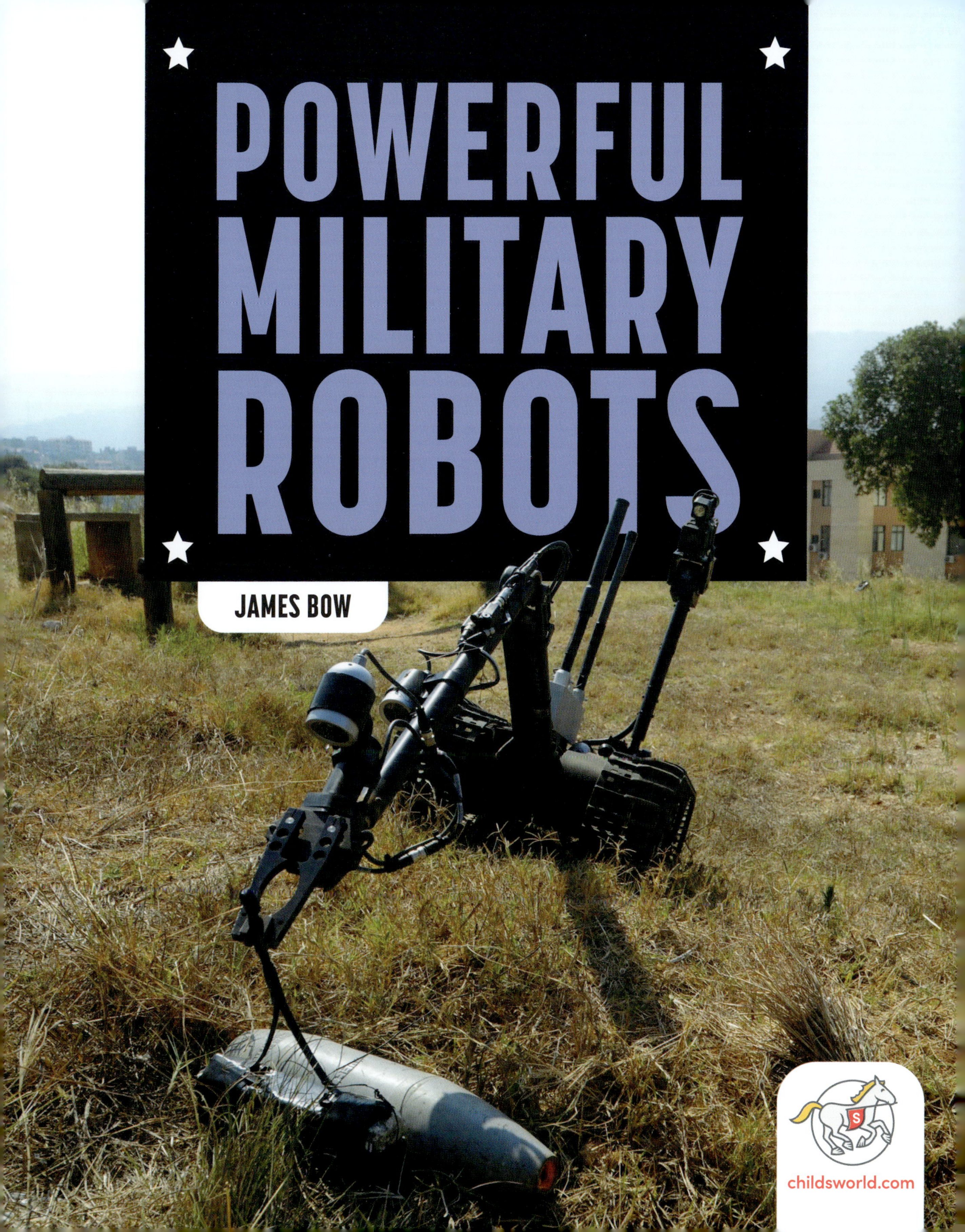

POWERFUL MILITARY ROBOTS

JAMES BOW

childsworld.com

Published by The Child's World®
800-599-READ • www.childsworld.com

Photography Credits
Photographs ©: Petty Officer 1st Class Joshua Scott/US Navy/DVIDS, cover, 1; Spc. Brandon D. Bolick/US Army/DVIDS, 3; Petty Officer 3rd Class Jacob Van Amburg/USS *George Washington* (CVN 73)/US Navy/DVIDS, 5; John Williams/US Navy/DVIDS, 6, 9; Samuel King Jr./96th Test Wing Public Affairs/US Air Force/DVIDS, 11; Bob Edme/AP Images, 13; Airman Joshua Maund/Joint Base Charleston Public Affairs/DVIDS, 15; Sgt. Sarah Anderson/US Marine Corps Forces, Pacific/DVIDS, 17; Airman Anabel Del Vall/325th Fighter Wing Public Affairs/US Air Force/DVIDS, 19; Mark Schauer/US Army Yuma Proving Ground/DVIDS, 21

ISBN Information
9781503816718 (Reinforced Library Binding)
9781503881396 (Portable Document Format)
9781503882706 (Online Multi-user eBook)
9781503884014 (Electronic Publication)

LCCN 2022951259

Printed in the United States of America

ABOUT THE AUTHOR

James Bow writes science fiction novels and nonfiction children's books. He's fascinated to see robots change from science fiction to science fact.

CONTENTS

CHAPTER ONE

SAFFiR

There's a fire on the ship! Alarms wail. Officers shout orders. Crew members hurry to find out what is happening. The sailors must act quickly. They don't want anyone to get hurt.

There has been an explosion in the ship's engine room. The walls and floors are damaged. The flames are intense. The fire safety system isn't working. The engine room is too hot for people to go in and fight the fire.

But the crew stays calm. The captain gives orders. Sailors near the fire turn on equipment. A robot marches forward, carrying a fire hose.

The Shipboard **Autonomous** Firefighting Robot (SAFFiR) was built for this. It stands on two legs. It weighs as much as a human. It has cameras in its head to see. But SAFFiR can go where people can't.

Sailors practice fire drills to make sure they know how to use equipment in case there is an emergency.

DCRS

PARTS OF SAFFiR

A camera sent sailors images of SAFFiR's surroundings. A heat-sensing camera saw through smoke. A gas sensor detected dangerous gases that could explode.

SAFFiR's arms could carry heavy objects. The robot could use a fire hose and a fire extinguisher.

SAFFIR's battery powered the robot for up to 30 minutes before it needed to be recharged.

SAFFiR's legs could climb over things on the ground better than if the robot had wheels.

Sensors told SAFFiR about its surroundings. It could walk over uneven or shaking floors.

At a command, SAFFiR walks through the narrow hallway. It stops by the door and turns. Its sensors detect the heat of the fire through the smoke.

SAFFiR lifts a fire hose and aims it at the source of the flames. It sprays a jet of water. The flames go out. As the smoke clears, sailors can enter in protective gear to bring out anyone who was injured.

The fire was not actually real. It was a test of the SAFFiR **prototype**. SAFFiR was built by engineers at Virginia Tech who were working with the US Navy. The robot was designed to walk through ship corridors. It could balance on rocking seas. Its robotic hands could grip a powerful fire hose. But SAFFiR was never used by the Navy. It was replaced with even more advanced robots.

SAFFiR's different parts allow it to help sailors in many ways. Its humanlike shape helps the robot work in spaces designed for humans.

★ ★ ★

Nadia is one of these powerful robots. It can do more than fight fires. Nadia will remove bombs from places that are too dangerous for humans. It may also respond to natural disasters. It could repair broken things on ships. Advanced robots will help soldiers work more efficiently and more safely.

Working in the military can be dangerous. But robots can help. They are designed with the newest technology. They can go into dangerous places without putting soldiers at risk. They can do simple tasks, allowing soldiers to focus on more important things. They can save lives.

SAFFiR and other emergency response robots are tested many times. Testing makes sure that robots can handle emergencies correctly.

CHAPTER TWO

RECONNAISSANCE ROBOTS

Soldiers sometimes use robots for **reconnaissance** missions. The military does reconnaissance to find out information such as an enemy's location. Soldiers might also need to learn about the **terrain** of an area. But this can be dangerous work. Enemies may be lying in wait. Traps may be set. Using robots can keep soldiers safe.

One reconnaissance robot is the Throwbot. This device has a sticklike body with one wheel on each side. It is about 8 inches (20 cm) long. Soldiers can throw the robot into a place to learn more about it. The Throwbot could be used on a battlefield or in an enemy base. The robot's small size makes it easy for soldiers to carry.

The Throwbot has two long antennae that help it send information back to a soldier's remote control.

Once the Throwbot lands, soldiers use a remote control to drive it. The robot has a camera that allows soldiers to see its surroundings. Its microphone picks up sounds. The Throwbot can drive through buildings to find enemies. It can check for traps such as hidden bombs. Soldiers can search an area without putting themselves in danger.

With **surveillance** robots, smaller is better. These robots can keep an eye on enemies without being seen. The Black Hornet is a tiny surveillance drone that looks like a helicopter. It fits in one hand and flies almost silently. It is especially useful in **urban** areas. The Black Hornet can fly through a window without being noticed. It sends soldiers live video of what it sees. Soldiers can spy on enemies without entering enemy territory. The Black Hornet can also be used to detect threats ahead while soldiers are on the move.

THE ROBOBEE

The RoboBee is even smaller than the Black Hornet. It is smaller than a paper clip. It weighs the same as a real bee. The RoboBee can carry a small camera or microphone. Since it's so small, the RoboBee isn't damaged if it runs into something. This technology makes the RoboBee useful and sturdy.

Thanks to robots, soldiers can explore their surroundings without putting themselves at risk. Troops can find and spy on enemies without being noticed. Reconnaissance robots give troops important information so they can stay safe.

A Black Hornet can fly for up to 25 minutes before it needs to be recharged.

CHAPTER THREE

SUPPORT ROBOTS

Robots do more than gather information. They also can complete tasks that are too difficult or dangerous for troops. The T7 is a robot that can handle many tough jobs. The US military uses it to **dispose** of bombs. The T7 can pick up bombs and move them away from any people before they explode.

The T7 looks like a mechanical arm attached to tank treads. The treads allow the T7 to drive across rough terrain. It can climb steep hills. This is useful if the robot is needed on the battlefield. It can even climb stairs. The T7 can go wherever it is needed.

Soldiers show the precision of the T7 by completing difficult tasks using its robotic arm.

HARRIS

The T7's robotic arm is easy to control. It has two cameras, so soldiers can see exactly what they are doing while they operate the arm. A claw allows the T7 to grab bombs and move them. The claw is so precise that it can do things such as open car doors and unzip zippers. This precision allows the T7 to access bombs in many locations. The claw can even sense pressure. The T7 can be gentle so bombs do not explode accidentally. The claw also has a tool to cut wires. Cutting wires may be necessary to **defuse** a bomb.

Robots help troops with other difficult jobs. In the 2010s, US Marines tested a walking robot made by Boston Dynamics to help soldiers carry heavy equipment across uneven ground. Soldiers often carry as much as 120 pounds (54 kg) of equipment on their backs. But the Legged Squad Support System (LS3) robot was created to help. The robot looked a bit like a large dog. It could carry more than 400 pounds (180 kg) of gear. It was programmed to follow troops as they moved along.

But the LS3 was too loud. Soldiers worried that enemies would hear them coming. The LS3 isn't used by the US military today. Boston Dynamics went on to create a new robot dog called Spot. Spot is smaller than the LS3. It can carry only 30 pounds (14 kg) of equipment. But it is a much more advanced robot. It can move more quickly and quietly than the LS3. The military can attach many kinds of sensors and cameras to Spot. It can be used for reconnaissance or to assist soldiers in battle. The design of Spot and robots like it will continue to be improved in the future.

The Legged Squad Support System could walk over difficult terrain. Sometimes, it would fall down. But the robot could usually stand up again on its own.

CHAPTER FOUR

COMBAT AND DEFENSE ROBOTS

The company Ghost Robotics makes robot dogs similar to Spot. In 2021, its new Q-UGV robot joined the US Air Force. But the Air Force did not send Q-UGV into battle. Instead, the robot became a guard dog. It can **patrol** the edges of an air base.

Q-UGV uses cameras and sensors to see its surroundings. It sends information back to soldiers. The Air Force uses the robotic guard dog to patrol areas of the base where people don't usually go. This allows soldiers to focus their attention on more important places. Future versions could let soldiers in camp speak through the robot to challenge intruders.

Q-UGV works in bad weather. It can cover rough terrain. These features make the robot helpful in difficult conditions.

Later in 2021, Ghost Robotics made an addition to Q-UGV. A gun was attached to the robot. The gun can hit targets about .75 miles (1.2 km) away. An armed robot could allow the military to fight from hard-to-reach locations. It could keep soldiers safe from enemy attack. However, the US military says that weapons must be controlled by humans. Q-UGV could not fire its gun without a human giving the command.

The US Army is adding a larger combat robot to its forces, too. The Optionally Manned Fighting Vehicle (OMFV) is a new kind of tank. It can be controlled remotely. The OMFV will work alongside troops in battle. It will add firepower without needing as many additional soldiers as would be necessary to operate a tank. The OMFV will help soldiers defeat enemy aircraft and other tanks.

AUTONOMOUS ROBOTS

Currently, most robots are operated by humans using remote controls. But militaries are developing robots that operate autonomously. By making decisions on their own, robots could respond to things around them faster than people could. They may be less likely to make mistakes. However, this ability also creates risks. If autonomous robots do make mistakes, a human may not be able to stop them. Developments in autonomous robots could change the way wars are fought in the future.

The US Army has tested technology for the Optionally Manned Fighting Vehicle on the Bradley Fighting Vehicle. These tests help engineers make the best-possible robot.

Military robots are designed to keep soldiers safe. They do simple jobs to allow humans to do other work. They take on dangerous tasks to save human lives. They gather information without being seen. Robots have become faster, stronger, and quieter. As technology becomes more advanced, robots will continue to take over more tasks.

GLOSSARY

autonomous (ah-TAH-nuh-mus) If something is autonomous, it can make decisions on its own. Autonomous robots can operate without a human controlling them.

defuse (deh-FYOOZ) To defuse a bomb means to stop the bomb from exploding. Robots can defuse bombs.

dispose (dih-SPOHZ) To dispose of something means to get rid of it. Robots can dispose of bombs by taking them far away from humans before letting them explode.

patrol (puh-TROHL) To patrol means to watch over an area, usually by walking around it regularly. Q-UGV can patrol parts of an air base so humans don't have to.

prototype (PROH-tuh-type) A prototype is something built to test a concept or a design. SAFFiR was a prototype the military built to test firefighting robots.

reconnaissance (reh-KON-nuh-suhns) Reconnaissance is exploring an area to learn about it and what is happening there. Robots can do reconnaissance to learn about an area before military forces move in.

surveillance (sur-VAY-lens) Surveillance is watching an area or person closely over time. Small robots like the Black Hornet can do surveillance without being seen.

terrain (tuh-RAYN) Terrain means an area of land and its natural features. Many military robots are designed to move easily over rough terrain.

urban (UR-buhn) Urban describes a city. A small, quiet robot is useful in an urban area.

FAST FACTS

- Robots can be used to do things that are too dangerous for humans to do.
- SAFFiR was a prototype robot for fighting fires. It looked a bit like a human, but it could go places humans could not.
- Soldiers use small robots such as the Throwbot and Black Hornet for reconnaissance. These robots gather information without being noticed.
- The T7 robot is used to defuse bombs. Spot is a doglike robot that can assist troops.
- The Optionally Manned Fighting Vehicle is a large combat robot. It looks like a tank and can be controlled remotely.
- Most robots are controlled by people from a distance. But militaries are designing robots that can make their own decisions.

ONE STRIDE FURTHER

- Think about the types of reconnaissance robots used by the military. What kinds of missions would each robot be best at? What robot features are most important for that mission?
- Should robots fight on the battlefield by themselves? How would this help soldiers? What problems might arise?
- Can you think of a new type of robot that could help soldiers? What would it do?

FIND OUT MORE

IN THE LIBRARY

Henzel, Cynthia Kennedy. *Powerful Military Drones.* Parker, CO: The Child's World, 2024.

Lindeen, Mary. *Law Enforcement Robots.* Minneapolis, MN: Lerner Publications, 2018.

Noll, Elizabeth. *Military Robots.* Minneapolis, MN: Bellwether Media, 2018.

ON THE WEB

Visit our website for links about powerful military robots:
childsworld.com/links

Note to Parents, Caregivers, Teachers, and Librarians: We routinely verify our Web links to make sure they are safe and active sites. So encourage your readers to check them out!

INDEX